A Fighting Chance: How to Rise After Severe Trauma

By Shannon Venita Roberts

TABLE OF CONTENTS

2 — Chapter 1
A Fighting Chance, Never Giving Up

6 — Chapter 2
Bouncing Back – Partying with a Purpose

9 — Chapter 3
Perspective of Praise

12 — Chapter 4
Fight for Focus

15 — Chapter 5
You Have the Right to Remain Silent

18 — Chapter 6
A Whole New World

21 — Chapter 7
Be in Action—Comfortably Uncomfortable

24 — Chapter 8
Pressing Forward

27 — Chapter 9
A Family Affair (Teamwork)

30 — Chapter 10
Battle Ready

32 — Chapter 11
Letting Go

36 — Chapter 12
Sight Unseen

39 — Chapter 13
There is Something about the Name of Jesus

42 — Chapter 14
Mindfulness

44 — Chapter 15
Knocked Down, but New Vision

47 — Chapter 16
Buckling Foundation

51 — Chapter 17
Rooted in Christ

54 — Chapter 18
Strategic strength

58 — Chapter 19
New Journey

62 — Chapter 20
Awareness

66 — Chapter 21
Overcomer

01

CHAPTER 01

A Fighting Chance, Never Giving Up

Life can change within a blink of an eye. It was the end of the week, and my divorce from my ex-husband was finalized at long last. My fight started when I went home for lunch. I opened my apartment door, and my ex-husband was waiting inside with a pistol. Somehow he had managed to get a key to my apartment. I went inside, and we began arguing. Then, he shot me in the back of the head. After being shot, I remember hearing a voice yelling at me in my head, telling me never to give up.

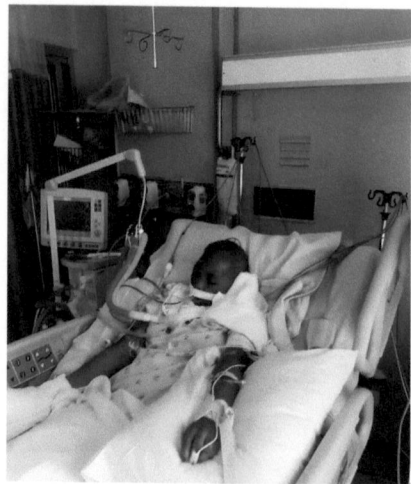

In addition, as a result of being shot, I also suffered a stroke. In combination, these two incidents caused me to have severe brain damage. After being cleared to leave the ICU, I wasn't moved to a regular hospital room. I required specialized care because I had a traumatic brain injury (TBI). The American Association of Neurological Surgeons (AANS) patient page posted the results of a recent U.S. study, which shows gunshot wounds to the head are the cause of an estimated 35% of all deaths attributed to TBI. Gunshot wounds to the head are fatal about 90% of the time, with victims often dying before arriving at the hospital. For victims who survive the initial trauma, about 50% die in the emergency room.

The Mayo Clinic describes a traumatic brain injury (TBI) as a bump, blow, or jolt to the head or a penetrating head injury that disrupts the normal function of the brain. A TBI can consist of, but is not limited to, the following categories: physical, cognitive, emotional, and behavioral symptoms.

There are vital systems associated with each TBI category. An individual may be affected differently to varying degrees, depending on the severity of their injury. I experienced all the categories, including the severe symptoms associated with each category as a result of being shot and suffering a stroke.

The right side of my skull was shattered. I lost the vision in my right eye because of a detached retina. Because of the stroke, I am paralyzed on my left side and my mobility has been affected. I now have to utilize a wheelchair. I lost the use of my leg and arm, my speech, and my ability to swallow.

The stroke caused a lot of physical and mental challenges, but I was up for the fight! Because of the severe trauma to my brain, I wasn't breathing correctly, so a temporary tracheostomy tube was surgically placed in my throat. Since I couldn't speak, I utilized a small whiteboard to communicate, but my handwriting wasn't legible. I wrote minutely because of the trauma.

So, to communicate, I was signaling with a thumbs up or thumbs down. Because I had trouble swallowing, I was placed on a pureed diet. All my food had to be ground, pressed, or strained to a smooth consistency, like pudding. I would joke to myself and say I was eating baby food again. It was to regroup. But I was taking baby steps!

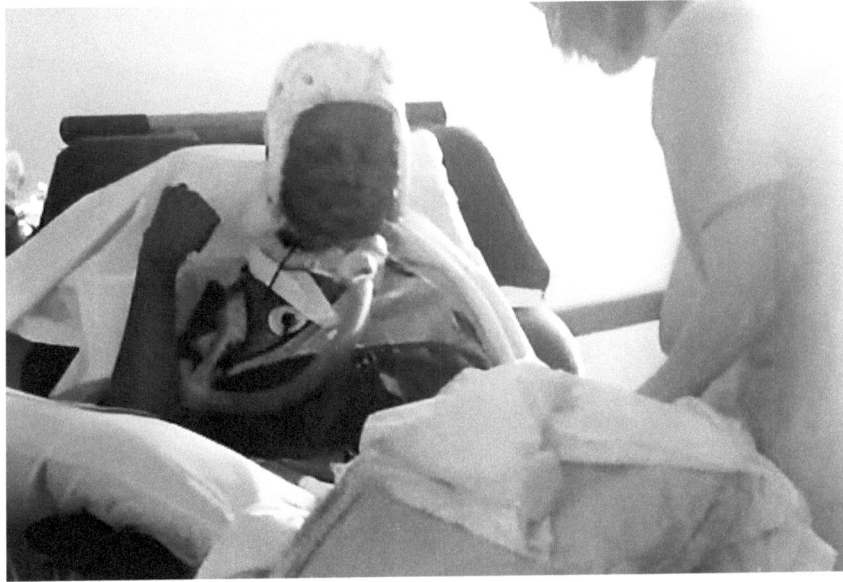

I had a great challenge to face. But with each step, no matter how big or small, I always knew that, with God's help, I would continue to grow stronger. The progress I was making was all thanks to Him.

To meet my nutritional needs, I had a feeding tube in my stomach. Yet I remembered John 6:35: "And Jesus said to them, 'I am the bread of life. He who comes to Me shall never hunger, and he who believes in Me shall never thirst.'" (NKJV) I knew I could feast on the bread of life and God's word and never go hungry. With any fight that came my way, I had a flow of everlasting blessings to provide me with everything I needed physically and mentally.

WORKSHEET

Use the space below to take action and journal about taking unique baby steps each day to achieve your current or future goals.

John 6:35: "*And Jesus said to them, 'I am the bread of life. He who comes to Me shall never hunger, and he who believes in Me shall never thirst.*"

02

CHAPTER 02

Bouncing Back – Partying with a Purpose

My life changed drastically, but I found an inner strength and peace to keep going: a strength deep within my soul. This strength lets you know and believe that everything will be fine. I had moments of a pity party for one—just myself—but I didn't party too long. During these parties, I tried to have the best food for thought.

We all need encouragement from time to time. The word of God in 1 Samuel 30:6 (KJV) says, "And David was greatly distressed; for the people spake of stoning him, because the soul of all the people was grieved, every man for his sons and for his daughters: but David encouraged himself in the LORD his God." Many times I had to speak victory and life into my situation by encouraging myself. I learned how to speak beyond my circumstances. I would always tell myself that I was amazing and proud of myself.

When I'm feeling down, I don't drink wine. Instead, I am filled by the Holy Spirit. The word of God states in Ephesians 5:18: "And do not be drunk with wine, in which is dissipation; but be filled with the Spirit." The Holy Spirit gave me peace and comfort.

I didn't like to party too long. I kept the depressed decorations to a minimum. I only have flowers and balloons. The flowers are reminders that even though I've experienced trauma, I'm still alive. I continue to grow stronger and receive healing because "He was wounded for our transgressions, He was bruised for our iniquities; the chastisement for our peace was upon Him, and by His stripes we are healed." Isaiah 53:5

The balloons create a scene of celebration; they encourage me to continue to soar and to keep fighting because life can change so fast and unexpectedly. I end my pity party by focusing on perspective. And, by doing this, I have learned to unwind – to enjoy every moment with gratitude and to appreciate the simple things in life.

Because I was on a pureed diet, I had to have the tracheostomy tube cleaned frequently, and the cleaning process was very uncomfortable. Over time, the doctors noticed I was doing well. I had always known and had faith that God would heal me. The doctors asked me if I wanted to have the tracheostomy tube removed. The doctor explained that after removing the tube, my oxygen levels would need to be at a certain level. If not, the tube had to be put back into my throat.

After the conversation about the process, I went into prayer. The Bible says in Philippians 4:6-7 "Be anxious for nothing, but in everything by prayer and supplication, with thanksgiving, let your requests be made known to God; and the peace of God, which surpasses all understanding, will guard your hearts and minds through Christ Jesus."

During the day, I didn't focus on my breathing. When it was time for the doctor to check my oxygen level, I was excited. When he checked my level, he informed me that my oxygen level exceeded the recommended level. I was reminded of 2 Corinthians 9:8, which assures us, "And God is able to make all grace abound toward you, that you, always having all sufficiency in all things, may have an abundance for every good work." God had not only given me enough. God supplied me with more than I needed.

Ephesians 5:18 "And do not be drunk with wine, in which is dissipation; but be filled with the Spirit."

Isaiah 53:5 "was bruised for our iniquities; the chastisement for our peace was upon Him, and by His stripes we are healed"

WORKSHEET

Take action and journal about what you are grateful for.

_____

_____

_____

_____

_____

_____

_____

_____

_____

_____

_____

Philippians 4:6-7 "Be anxious for nothing, but in everything by prayer and supplication, with thanksgiving, let your requests be made known to God; and the peace of God, which surpasses all understanding, will guard your hearts and minds through Christ Jesus."

Corinthians 9:8 " which assures us, "And God is able to make all grace abound toward you, that you, always having all sufficiency in all things, may have an abundance for every good work."

CHAPTER 03

Perspective of Praise

I've realized life is all about your perspective. Things had drastically changed for me—even to do the normal, simple things I did in the past.

After a few weeks, I was finally shown my face and I was shocked because I barely recognized my face. He explained to me everything he could do to repair my shattered skull. In addition, he explained about losing my eye. I no longer had a muscle in that area of my eye, and my forehead was shattered. My eyelid was drooping halfway past my eye.

As I listened to what the doctor was saying, I had a feeling of disbelief and amazement. He also explained to me that I had serious cognitive issues. I'm sitting on a hospital bed looking at my face; holding a hand-held mirror, I'm looking at myself. When I first saw my head—no surgery, no bandages, just missing half of a skull—I was in complete shock and disbelief. After the doctor's explanation, I told him that I understood everything about my injury but I was mainly grateful to be alive. And all of this—my head and face—is superficial, and the main thing that matters is that I am still alive after being shot in the head.

Because I'm fearfully and wonderfully made. I was shocked, but I knew it was God who kept me. I knew that, to keep the devil from filling my head with the 'what ifs,' I now had to stay focused on God and not on the world.

Psalm 139:14 "I will praise You, for I am fearfully and wonderfully made; Marvelous are Your works, And that my soul knows very well."

Chapter 3: Perspective of Praise

WORKSHEET

Take action and journal about how you keep a positive perspective when dealing with difficulties.

04

CHAPTER 04

Fight for Focus

After seeing my now-disfigured face, I was extremely shocked about my new situation. I realized that my fight would also include my focus. When I thought about my face, I realized I was focusing on how the world would treat me. Thinking solely on that, I saw only the scars and the disarray. I was selfish, asking myself how I could now live in such a condition and how I would deal with all the medical attention I would need.

Then I thought about how I could no longer play the piano with only one hand, and I forgot that God calls me beautiful because he created me. I finally realized I had to continue setting my focus only on Jesus.

As a former church musician, I always kept a song in my mouth. One of my favorite hymns to recite during my quiet, still moments is "Father, I stretch my hand to thee. No other help I know. If Thou withdraw Thy hand from me, O whither shall I go?" The Scripture I kept in my heart was Isaiah 26:3: "You will keep him in perfect peace, Whose mind is stayed on You, Because he trusts in You." I had to stay focused on God and not on the world.

Isaiah 26:3 "You will keep him in perfect peace, Whose mind is stayed on You, Because he trusts in You"

WORKSHEET

Take action and journal about some areas (personal or business) where you can change your focus from overthinking situations.

05

CHAPTER 05

You Have the Right to Remain Silent

WORKSHEET

Take action and journal about how uncontrollable situations can be silent hindrances.

06

CHAPTER 06

A Whole New World

WORKSHEET

Take action and journal about small things you can change to make yourself more available to pursue your hopes and dreams.

07

CHAPTER 07

Be in Action—Comfortably Uncomfortable

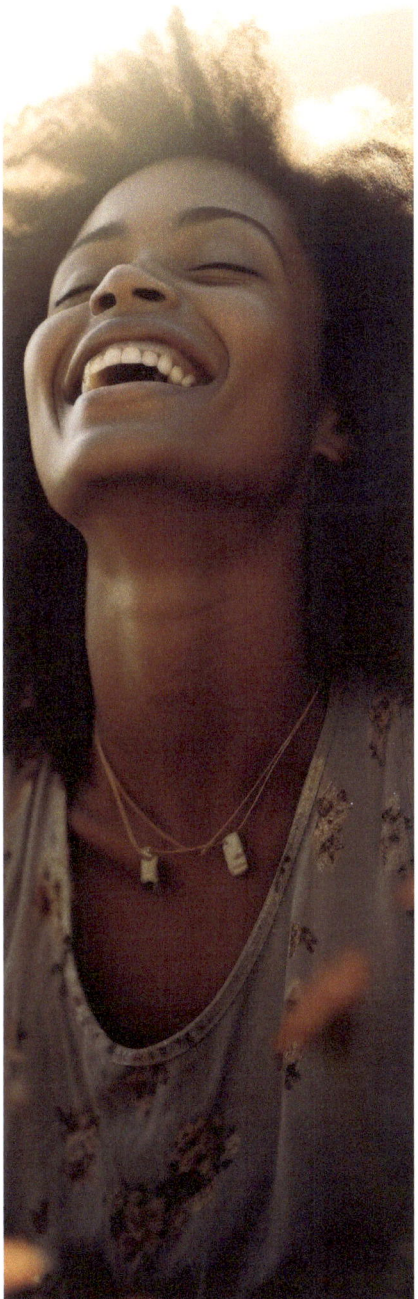

It's the simple things we take for granted. I was now missing and appreciated the simplicity of being able to handle any situation. I was certain of that.

Dressing and bathing myself without assistance was no longer an option for me. I was very uncomfortable with someone else having to wash me. Tying my shoes consisted of me pushing a button and waiting for assistance. I was in my early forties and thought those years had ended a long, long time ago. I had thought I had a few more years and grey hairs before I would need that type of care.

Many times, my mind wanted to think about the negative aspects of everything. But when that happened, I had to change my focus and think about all the positive things in my life. I now found myself being comfortably uncomfortable. Life can change so unexpectedly. But God has a plan and purpose for everything. I used to get so upset with trying to put on a jacket with only one arm, so I would wear it over my shoulders instead of dealing with the frustration.

Jeremiah 29:11 "For I know the plans I have for you, saith the Lord. Plans to prosper you and not to harm you; plans to give you a hope and a future."

WORKSHEET

Pause and reflect on a time when you felt comfortably uncomfortable. In addition, reflect on what techniques you can use to help fight those feelings when they overwhelm you.

08

CHAPTER 08

Pressing Forward

To adjust to being away from home, in unfamiliar surroundings with a new lifestyle, I decided I had to press forward with my new, beautiful life ahead. In doing so, I found strength through prayer, gratitude, and appreciation.

I kept pushing myself to keep fighting. Simple things gave me a fighting chance. I decided to try different activities that the facilities offered. Going outside and feeling the sun on my skin felt like a beam of happiness from heaven. The Word of God says true happiness is found in Jesus Christ. Psalm 144:15 (NKJV): "Happy are the people who are in such a state; Happy are the people whose God is the Lord!"

Even though I had a lot of physical and cognitive challenges, my genuine happiness was found in Jesus Christ. So I was pressing forward because I realized being happy is a choice. And simple things like putting on a jacket by myself gave me joy and assurance.

I was speaking more and learning more and my cognitive problems were getting better. I found happiness within myself. During one activity, we were working on the computer. I've always enjoyed working on the computer. During the activity, the instructor noticed I was doing well. So, I created a flier for an upcoming event. I was pressing forward.

I planted a flower and, on the flower pot, I wrote the words "sunshine every day." I would look at the plant and think 'My life is like this flower. I'm growing and getting stronger, flourishing daily.' I started competing with myself to do better daily by thinking about all the positive things I'd accomplished and overcome so far.

I started regrouping from my severe trauma by subtracting all my negative thoughts. I realized it was mind over matter. I started adding appreciation to my life.

WORKSHEET

Journal about a time when you had to press forward by subtracting from your comfort zone to accomplish a task.

CHAPTER 09

A Family Affair (Teamwork)

I was now strong enough to go to a rehabilitation facility back home without the assistance of an ambulance. I was able to ride in a vehicle. I still had my feeding tube and half of a skull, but I was alive and getting better and stronger.

When I was away doing therapy, I knew my fight and the reality of having my rights removed still existed. Going back home meant I had to face the situation head-on. I had to be headstrong. Being back home brought about more fights because I was declared incapacitated and my rights had been removed.

I found myself fighting in another big fight. I had to fight to decide the welfare of my children. Having to testify in court about the welfare of my children took a lot of strength, especially since I was still adjusting to my new lifestyle. Now, my children also had to adjust to a new lifestyle, but we all remained God-strong. My children and I all decided that we would utilize some form of therapy to help us deal with the current situation.

Prayer was still our first form of assurance, but sometimes you need additional assistance to help you cope with trauma. This fight had a big cost associated with the team. I was victorious and everyone on the team was happy with the outcome. Knowing my boys were with family who cared about them filled me with peace.

Because my cognitive issues had improved, and I could communicate better, I inquired about restoring my rights. This process involved a tedious battle, which I had to fight on several occasions.

WORKSHEET

Take a moment to journal about adding motivation to learn and grow through challenges.

CHAPTER 10

Battle Ready

Surgery time was quickly approaching. I was nervous and excited at the same time, even though I knew trust and anxiety could not exist together. I was excited! Because of my shattered skull, I had to wear a helmet, even though it offered minimal coverage for my fragile head.

I also had to wear a different type of helmet to defeat and battle against the supernatural fights of this world as well. To defeat the devil, sometimes I had to armor up for whatever form the attacks came in. I was battle-ready, for I was always protected by God's armor found in Ephesians 6:10-18 (KJV):

"Finally, my brethren, be strong in the Lord, and in the power of his might. Put on the whole armor of God, that ye may be able to stand against the wiles of the devil. For we wrestle not against flesh and blood, but against principalities, against powers, against the rulers of the darkness of this world, against spiritual wickedness in high places. Wherefore take unto you the whole armor of God, that ye may be able to withstand in the evil day, and having done all, to stand. Stand therefore, having your loins girt about with truth, and having on the breastplate of righteousness; And your feet shod with the preparation of the gospel of peace; Above all, taking the shield of faith, wherewith ye shall be able to quench all the fiery darts of the wicked. And take the helmet of salvation, and the sword of the Spirit, which is the word of God: Praying always with all prayer and supplication in the Spirit, and watching thereunto with all perseverance and supplication for all."

Jesus has won the ultimate victory. To protect myself from attacks, I only had to armor up when the enemy attacked saints.

God had given me all the necessary equipment to fight the spiritual fight. Jesus has won the ultimate victory. When the devil tried to weigh down my life with his lies concerning my situation or any situation, I put on the belt of truth—God's truth about my life—I went to battle daily. I got ready to battle any situation and fight when I put on the belt of truth. Then I could go undefeated because God's truth about my life was secure.

Another essential and strong resource that God had given me was the breastplate of righteousness. I used it to block all the evil arrows the devil and his evil forces would throw at me in an attempt to invade my heart. It was there to keep my heart dedicated to God. Along with the breastplate I used the sword of the Spirit, which is the word of God. When God's Word is spoken, the devil is defeated. He gave me the strength to use this armor and sword.

When trials come, He helps me use the shield of faith. He gave me the shield of faith to strengthen me. v

My heavenly Father provides me with the best footwear! I was moving in peace against the devil because I was being led by God with the preparation of the gospel of peace (peace), the shield of faith, the helmet of salvation, and the sword of the Spirit (Word of God). Jesus has won the ultimate battle for us already. Daily I made sure I had on my outfit to fight—the armor of God. Each piece is rooted in a divine design by God as a resource to help fight the battles I had to face.

Take a moment to read Ephesians 6:10–18 and put on the full armor of God before going any further. Do this every day!

CHAPTER 11

Letting Go

I was nervous when I thought about skull surgery that I needed to have, but I found comfort in remembering Nehemiah 8:10 (KJV): For the joy of the LORD is your strength." after months of therapy and getting stronger mentally and physically it was now time to have my surgery to replace my skull and to lift my drooping eyelid. I had two doctors operating on me at the same time.

On the day of my surgery, I remember calling my prayer warriors to pray before I went into my head surgery. The last thing I remember before I was completely under anesthesia was the surgeon asking me if I wanted him to cut all of my hair off or just half. I decided only on the side where the surgery would take place. For some reason, I wanted to hold onto the other side of my hair, instead of cutting off the hair and allowing my hair to grow back stronger and healthier.

During that time, I realized my life was like longer hair. At times, we want to hold onto certain things in life that no longer serve us any purpose, instead of cutting off certain actions and behaviors for God to help us grow better by eliminating the ends hindering your growth. I had to cut off fear and replace it with faith. I had to cut out doubt and let hope grow instead. I had to cut off sadness and let joy grow instead.

When I finally awoke, I had to remain in the intensive care unit (ICU) until I was able to function more independently without the assistance of all the machines again and able to transfer from one position to the next without assistance. My right damaged eye with the detached retina was sewn shut. I had a new plastic skull and I had all these machines attached to my head.

On several occasions, I would look at the huge tubes connected to my head and, in another machine, I could see fluids going through the tubes. But I remained thankful and grateful and felt so blessed that I was still alive. I was determined to keep fighting because God is on my side and with God in my corner, I will always win.

I was finally able to transfer from one position to the next. I was transferring from the bed to my wheelchair. Being able to transfer safely was very important for me because, on the left side, I was paralyzed and I had a higher risk of falling, causing more damage. My confidence and endurance were getting stronger, especially since I was originally afraid of the surgery.

I was reminded of God's word in Hebrews 12:1-2 (NKJV): "Therefore we also, since we are surrounded by so great a cloud of witnesses, let us lay aside every weight, and the sin which so easily ensnares us, and let us run with endurance the race that is set before us, looking unto Jesus, the author and finisher of our faith, who for the joy that was set before Him endured the cross, despising the shame, and has sat down at the right hand of the throne of God."

My surgeon was amazed at how fast I was healing. I was just the vessel, but all the prayer and praise went to my heavenly Father, who had been on my side. No more staples and tubes in my head. The time had arrived when I was finally able to move from the ICU to a regular hospital room. When I got settled in my new room, I wanted to make sure I didn't lose any of the abilities I fought hard to regain again. I asked if I could start therapy again.

I was still fighting and wanted to make sure that I did not lose any mobility from the complicated surgery. I started therapy again because I did not feel safe walking by myself. Therapy kept the safety belt around my waist, even though before my surgery I was walking without assistance. But now, even though I had my new plastic skull eyelid lifted, I still had the detached retina. My eye couldn't be saved, but I was fine about that because I knew who protected me. I was also fearful and didn't feel secure walking by myself. But when I let go of the fear and focused on God, I started walking further in confidence. God's word says in Proverbs 30:5 (NKJV), "Every word of God is pure; He is a shield to those who put their trust in Him." My recovery was going very well after a few weeks in a regular hospital room. I still had a few stitches, but I was allowed to go home to finish healing.

WORKSHEET

Take action and journal about what you would do if you had the opportunity to do something impulsive.

CHAPTER 12

Sight Unseen

My cognitive issues significantly improved before I departed from the facility. I was now under the care and assistance of my family. I already knew that I had lost half of a skull and had only one eye, yet slowly but surely, I started to discover those were not the only things I lost. I was alive, but my way of living had changed. I was now in a fight to keep my financial affairs in order since I was declared incapacitated and required a guardian to handle all my affairs.

During this fight I was hit with more and more financial blows, and, with every blow, I dwindled. My new training area kept me locked away, but when officials needed to know my ("the Ward's") progress and condition status. Everything always seemed to measure and add up correctly on paper. When the ward eligibility and status were accepted and approved by the officials and judges, the financial and mental match started again. This time, it was longer and the financial hits started to get bigger, stronger, and faster.

Everyone felt they could cover up my lack of training. But, ultimately, I was still a ward of the court, required to adhere to guardianship, and still unfamiliar with the process. One morning I went to therapy, and when I came back from therapy, I was greeted by several individuals at the family home where I was staying after my surgery. The individuals came inside and asked me different social, legal, mental, financial, and physical questions. I was able to answer a few of the questions. My best response came when asked about my ability to groom my hair. I silently chuckled twice because I thought it was funny to have this assessment right after a long day of therapy. My big chuckle came when I removed the hood from my head. I looked at everyone and said, "Ma'am, to answer your question. I don't have any hair." There was a moment of silence. Then I just gently placed the hood back on my head.

A few weeks passed and I was informed that I did not score high enough to have my rights restored. I was disappointed and upset because I wasn't aware of the assessment day or time, but I kept a positive attitude. I knew the process for restoring my rights and, soon I knew what to expect.

After being hit with so many blows, and knowing I had to adhere to the guardian and the court rules and regulations, mentally I wanted to throw in the towel. Day by day, I stayed positive by knowing that, "With God, no weapon formed against me will prosper."

And I thank God for protecting and helping me, and always fighting my battles. And because I'm under God's guidance and leadership, no matter the circumstances, situation, or fight, I trusted and knew God was with me in every battle.

During the times when my head was held down, I found assurance from Jeremiah 29:11 (NKJV): "For I know the plans I have for you," declares the Lord, "plans to prosper you and not to harm you, plans to give you hope and a future." And when I was weary or uncertain, God was there to pick me up.

Isaiah 54:17, "No weapon formed against you shall prosper, And every tongue which rises against you in judgment You shall condemn. This is the heritage of the servants of the Lord, And their righteousness is from Me," says the Lord.

WORKSHEET

Take action and journal about a situation that has disappointed you the most. Also, include how your strengths helped you overcome the situation.

CHAPTER 13

There is Something about the Name of Jesus

While living with family I continued home therapy. Being home made the time go by fast and in no time, it seemed, it was time to have my stitches removed by my surgery doctor.

The day had arrived — the stitches were being removed from my head. I remember asking the doctor several questions about pain. I've had stitches before, but none in such a delicate and important area as the head. As the doctor removed several thick stitches, I was gripping my pants and calling on the name of Jesus.

Calling on the name of Jesus gives you strength and power to handle any and all situations. The name of Jesus can calm the most raging storm, no more bandages or stitches. I was home healing, but I was also home hiding from the world. Physically, I was able to get out and move around, but, mentally, I wasn't ready to face others besides my regulars, whom I was familiar and comfortable with. I now had to battle my thoughts and what I was thinking. Negative self-talk is a hard battle to fight.

I would tell myself that people would be focused and stare at my eye, or my head, or my scar. In real life, I was missing half of a skull. I had a plate. To me, it did not look perfect like the other side. I also didn't want people to be shocked that I was in a wheelchair now and paralyzed on one side. I had to silence the negative voices by having a lot of quiet moments with God and reading and meditating on God's word. Additionally, I changed and exchanged my attitude of heaviness for gladness and appreciation. I also had to question myself and ask myself where the thoughts were coming from.

Isaiah 61:3 (NKJV): To console those who mourn in Zion, to give them beauty for ashes, the oil of joy for mourning, the garment of praise for the spirit of heaviness; that they may be called trees of righteousness, The planting of the Lord, that He may be glorified.

WORKSHEET

Take action and write down positive traits they will adapt to counter negative self-talk.

14

CHAPTER 14

Mindfulness

Over time, the mind is one of the biggest challenges to overcome. One of my favorite scriptures I use as a guide for mindfulness is found in Philippians 4:8, "Finally, brethren, whatever things are true, whatever things are noble, whatever things are just, whatever things are pure, whatever things are lovely, whatever things are of good report, if there is any virtue and if there is anything praiseworthy—meditate on these things." In Hebrew, the definition of meditate means to muse or rehearse in one's mind. No matter what happened in my life, I had to focus my mind and thoughts regularly on thinking about the goodness of God. In addition, no matter the circumstances in which I lost a lot, I will always have Jesus and never give up living in God's strength. Besides, God was doing something new to get the victory in my life. I was knocking out negativity for positivity to prevail. That's what happened when I allowed the new thing in my life to contribute toward my fight for mindfulness.

I look at the lovely scar from my eye to the middle of one side of my head. Now say I have a tattoo sculpted by God's amazing grace. I remember lying in bed and I heard God's voice whispering. He told me to get up and to stop hiding. When I stopped listening to the negative voices in my head that were putting me down, I started living a life filled with more hope and faith. I began going out more, walking in confidence.

Just when I started experiencing life again with my new skull, I was hit with another punch. I suffered a seizure that hospitalized me. While in the hospital, I was informed that most people who have a traumatic brain injury (TBI) will have epilepsy seizures. A majority of the people with epilepsy will have this problem for their whole lives. However, the seizures are managed by medication and, because of medication management, I could return to most activities. No matter what new battles or events I have to fight or face, God is with me, and the battle is won. Because my situation had changed, instead of going back home when I was released from the hospital, I went back to my previous rehabilitation facility. I was determined to never give up, even though my situation and hindrances tried to weigh me down. Many days I would think about everything I've overcome and knew that God had kept me. The race that was set before me was great, but I had to keep running with endurance.

Take a moment to read Hebrews 12:1-2: "Therefore, since we are surrounded by so great a cloud of witnesses, let us also lay aside every weight, and sin which clings so closely, and let us run with endurance the race that is set before us, looking to Jesus, the founder and perfecter of our faith, who for the joy that was set before him endured the cross, despising the shame, and is seated at the right hand of the throne of God." Focus on God, run the race that He has set for you, and let Him take the weight off your shoulders.

CHAPTER 15

Knocked Down, but New Vision

Many of the staff members remembered me from before. They noticed something was different about me—I was no longer wearing my helmet! The old was gone. I was the same person; I just had a distinct vision and walk now. I meditated on Psalm 119:105 (NKJV): "Your word is a lamp to my feet, and a light to my path." I was back in rehabilitation after my seizure, but I was happier and stronger, mentally and physically.

After the last battle knocked me down for a moment and hospitalized me, I was back up now, stronger than ever before, and I had a new vision for my life. I had a new attitude and was ready to conquer any fights I had to face. I was never giving up. I was determined to thrive and survive after my severe trauma.

The time had finally come to have my feeding tube removed and I was so thankful. I was excited—my new beautiful life was ahead. All my scars were healing. Knowing that I now had to deal with seizures was a blow to me. Many times, having to deal with the physical issues was a lot to handle, but I wasn't giving up. I was determined never to give up. Many times it was hard to deal with, but I still had a fighting chance.

I was enjoying rehabilitation and was getting stronger. I was now doing activities of daily living more independently.

A few months later, I discovered I had another fight. Instead of enjoying my new place to reside in, which I was familiar with, having my rights removed and being declared incapacitated resurfaced again. I was told by my guardian that I could no longer live at the rehabilitation facility, but my guardian informed me she had found a place for me to live. It was at an adult care facility. Since I was declared incapacitated and had no rights, I had no decision or voice to determine my residence.

WORKSHEET

Take action and journal about a time you had to deal with any setback.

16

CHAPTER 16

Buckling Foundation

I met the owners of the adult healthcare house only once, but, within a few weeks, I was moving from the rehabilitation facility and being relocated with other adults I had never met before. In addition, the house was out of the way for my friends and family—another blow—but God kept me. The home structure was completely different from what I was used to from previous places where I resided. With each blow I was being hit, my mindset was one of a champion and I kept fighting.

The house structure wasn't entirely grounded and secure; the foundation was still being completed and stabilized. My spiritual structure was growing, especially since God is my master builder and my foundation was being built with precious stones of hope, faith, determination, and purpose. Because I always knew it was "on Christ, my solid rock, I stand and all other ground is sinking sand." One particular verse in the Bible that is my favorite when the Scripture speaks about building is Luke 6:48 (KJV): "He is like a man which built a house, and dug deep, and laid the foundation on a rock: and when the flood arose, the stream beat vehemently upon that house, and could not shake it: for it was founded upon a rock."

My physical structure took a small blow. I was having trouble walking because of my knee. Likewise, my financial situation was changing, with some things being outside my control. I was now responsible for all the additional personal items I needed. Because of this structure, I started receiving a monthly cash allowance for my expenses. With the allowance, I thought I could manage my own money, but I found out the guardian set a certain amount for me for the entire month, and then my guardian would manage everything else.

I had no idea how anything was being managed. This was a hard situation for me to handle. In addition, the allowance situation wasn't managed well. On several occasions, I had to contact my guardian about my allowance. I thank God for my family and friends who helped with my additional expenses when my guardian wasn't available.

To improve my walking, since I was in a different environment, I started therapy. While walking, my therapist noticed my knee was buckling when I was walking. To correct the issue, she required me to wear an even larger brace than what I was already wearing, which was currently only a few inches above my ankle. My new brace was heavier and reached up my leg to my thigh. The brace is larger because it locks my knee into place, preventing my knee from hyperextending without the brace. I was at a greater risk of falling. When I first started using the brace, I required assistance with putting on the brace. Because of my determination, I asked the therapist if they could teach me to put the brace on myself. And we did—we came up with a way for me to put on the brace myself. Another achievement!

I was a fighter; I was thankful, grateful, blessed, and never giving up. Now with my new brace, I walked more and started challenging myself to do more. I started walking up and down the stairs and going outside more. My thinking had changed because of my severe trauma. Every fight was fought with a new perspective. I remember one day looking at my wheelchair and saying to myself that my wheelchair does not define me. Everyone focused on my injuries, and yes, they were serious. But I focused on Joshua 1:9 (NKJV): "Have I not commanded you? Be strong and of good courage; do not be afraid, nor be dismayed, for the Lord your God is with you wherever you go."

I am courageous and I am God-strong. I am determined and powerful. I am not a ward of the courts. I am a daughter of my heavenly Father, and I am loved. I can face any situation because I am abiding in Christ and producing spiritual fruit that's found in God's word in Galatians 5:22-23 (NKJV): "But the fruit of the Spirit is love, joy, peace, long-suffering, kindness, goodness, faithfulness, gentleness, self-control. Against such there is no law." I was growing in Christ.

WORKSHEET

Take action and journal about circumstances others use to define you. In addition, use at least 8 adjectives to describe yourself.

CHAPTER 17

Rooted in Christ

My life had changed tremendously, but with everything, no matter what, I was determined to be victorious and not the victim. Just when I started to get comfortable with the new structure, I was dealt another blow—I was informed by my guardian that the house structure no longer met my official guardianship court requirements. I could no longer live there; I had to move again. And, once again, my guardian found me another facility. This place was very unique. Throughout my entire situation, I kept telling myself everything would be fine and that God was in control, so all was well. Because I'm rooted in Christ, no matter where I had to live, I found peace through prayer.

My entire situation hurt a lot, and I regrouped by being rooted in Christ daily. One particular scripture I focused on was Ephesians 3: 17: "So that Christ may dwell in your hearts through faith. And I pray that you, being rooted and established in love " Take action and journal about methods you use to keep yourself grounded during rough, shaky situations. There was no need for me to worry about my physical dwelling because of my faith. Christ was at home in my heart. God's love was rooted in my life, and this helped me realize I didn't have to worry about anything. I knew God had me. He sits high and looks down below; he sees everything.

Ephesians 3: 17 "so that Christ may dwell in your hearts through faith. And I pray that you, being rooted and established in love "

WORKSHEET

CHAPTER 18

Strategic strength

I wasn't happy about moving again to another facility. Once again, a decision was made on my behalf. Even though it was a touchy situation I had to accept, I continued to find peace from the Word of God. Philippians 4:11 (NKJV) states: "Not that I speak in regard to need, for I have learned in whatever state I am, to be content." Even though the new facility promoted more independence, this facility was unique for me because I was the youngest resident. Being the youngest was an interesting situation to handle.

Because of my trauma, I had to deal with a lot of other situations that could've left me feeling defeated. Instead, I decided to be happy because being happy is a choice.

"You have to make the most out of the deck of cards life deals you." Famous words spoken by Jacquez Daniels.

I was once again relocating to a living environment that met the court's requirements. In the game of life, you must have a strategy for every card you are dealt. By having a game plan to handle any severe trauma you face, and believing with a positive mindset that everything will be fine, you can overcome any obstacle.

Because of my limited income and other monthly obligations, my guardian could only make partial payments to the facility. I've always known that the partial payments were not enough to keep me at the facility. Eventually, management would hit me by requiring us to pay the full outstanding balance or I had to leave the facility. But during those times, I was reminded of Psalm 112:7 (NKJV): "They will have no fear of bad news; their hearts are steadfast, trusting in the Lord." Every day I continued with my normal activity. I did not focus on my situation or problems. My unwavering faith stayed focused on Jesus and helped me triumph over every battle I had to confront. I stayed strong in the Lord because I knew God was fighting my battles. I trusted and knew God was with me in every battle that I had to fight. And when I was weary or uncertain, God was there to pick me up.

What you are holding onto means you will have a fighting chance. But no matter what the cards deal you in the game of life, there is no greater teacher than experience. Home therapy worked well for me previously, but now the facility had a therapy room and a structured therapy program. To reach my full potential, I decided to start therapy again. I improved tremendously. I could now shower myself, which was a big victory for me. I was able to have another guardian assessment evaluation. This time I scored much higher. The assessment is just a portion of the process of having my rights restored. My attorney had to file a petition with the local courts. Once the petition was filed, a hearing was scheduled and a judge would determine whether my rights would be restored.

Romans 8:37 (NKJV): Yet in all these things we are more than conquerors through Him who loved us.

Time passed and I finally received my hearing date. During the hearing, the judge asked my current guardian and me questions. In addition, he discussed the components of the assessment, in which I scored low in certain areas, particularly math. The judge decided a guardian was still required to oversee my financial affairs. I no longer had a full guardian; I now had a limited guardian. According to Chapter 744 of the Florida statutes, a limited guardian means a guardian who has been appointed by the court to exercise the legal rights and powers specifically designated by a court order entered after the court has found that the ward can do some, but not all, of the tasks necessary to care for his or her person or property, or after the person has voluntarily petitioned for appointment of a limited guardian. Many of my rights were restored, but because I still required a guardian, I was still considered a ward of the court. A plan was put into place to have my rights restored shortly. The plan involved me strengthening my weak areas. I immediately developed a strategy to overcome those areas.

Before I saw my improvement, I thought I was fighting a losing battle because I focused on the problem and not God, the provider. In the game of life, you learn a great deal from your wins and losses. The new facility was a win for me. I started using the wheelchair less and I started using a walker. Later, I started using a cane instead and walking farther distances. The main objective of the game of life during trauma is to keep fighting and, with God's help, keep winning.

The current director at the facility was aware of my financial battles and had a payment arrangement plan with my guardian. Things were going well, then I was incidentally slapped with another obstacle: the facility hired a new director. The old director was familiar with my financial situation, but with a new director, changes happened. I was now faced with the fear and the challenge of the unknown.

"Fear is the biggest disability of all, it will paralyze you more than being in a wheelchair." - Nick Vujicic.

I decided that, as new challenges came my way, I wasn't going to be crippled by fear. Especially since I trusted God completely. To help me meet each challenge head-on with wisdom and guidance, I decided to face all the challenges and fights in my life with courage. I refuse to be paralyzed by fear and have faith instead. I know God is always with me during each new journey, so I have the victory. During each fight I have to face—with God's help, I have no fear and can flourish because God has called me to be strong. He helps me conquer difficult obstacles, because I am more than a conqueror.

WORKSHEET

Take action and journal about your praiseworthy aspects and shortcomings.

CHAPTER 19

New Journey

The time had arrived. I was finally hit with the past with my many financial punches. We received a letter letting us know I had to leave the facility by a certain day. Since I now had some of my rights restored, I could select my own living arrangements. I thought my first option would be to choose a housing facility that was set up for the disabled. I made several calls, but many handicap-accessible places had a one-year waiting period. And time was of the essence.

I decided to change my thinking. I knew I was much stronger and only needed a few special accommodations. My search changed and I started looking for apartments with handicap accessibility. I found a place that could and would accommodate the additional changes I needed. In addition, my place is closer to family and friends and is closer to town than my previous facility.

My moving day was exciting and scary. I had become accustomed to being around residents and staff. Now I was starting a new journey. God had always been with me, and He was leading and guiding me all the way. I would be on my own now, but never alone. I found strength and comfort in Psalm 27:1 ESV: "The Lord is my light and my salvation; whom shall I fear? The Lord is the stronghold of my life—of whom shall I be afraid?"

All my items and I were moved and relocated to my new apartment. All my special accommodations were made; the only thing missing was me.

Once everyone finished getting me situated and I stopped organizing everything, I had to give God all the praise and honor. I broke down and cried tears of happiness. I thought about how I've cried so many tears of disappointment and hurt. I had to endure mental and physical pain that no one could see. Only God saw the tears I carried until I couldn't handle them, so I completely surrendered everything to God. I finally decided that I, by myself, was fighting a losing battle. During the times when I lay awake at night, wondering if anything would change, I pondered why things had to happen.

But God reminded me many times that He is in control.

I tried to organize everything, but I couldn't because I was so thankful and grateful that my trauma did not defeat me. I had to keep stopping to lift my hands in praise. I kept the faith, even when I did not understand the process or had no one to call and talk to. I knew God had a purpose and plan for everything.

I finally got everything situated a little before I went to bed. I couldn't stop praising and thanking God. Because I was so filled with praise and worship, I decided the next day was the day I would finish unpacking everything.

Every morning, I always had a special prayer I prayed, but now my prayer was different. I thought about the time when I once awoke to tubes in my head and being connected to several monitoring machines. Daily I thanked God for keeping me in my right mind.

My daily schedule did not change much. I was now responsible for preparing my own meals, which I was excited about. I enjoy cooking and washing dishes. I now had to factor into my schedule meal preparation. I'm always careful since I was now on my own and had to depend more on other people.

My attitude started changing. Frustration was now my friend and I didn't want the friendship because I was becoming irritated more often. And my tone of speech—I noticed I became angry more easily. I was sarcastic or snapping at individuals verbally. My situation had changed for the better. I became aware of my behavior and immediately decided I needed to improve. I first started by talking to my therapist. I became aware of behavior that wasn't reflecting my praise and worship as a daughter of my heavenly Father.

WORKSHEET

Take an assessment of your current situation, then take the time and journal about what makes you feel positive about the future.

CHAPTER 20

Awareness

After I became aware of my behavior and wasn't pleased with myself, I decided to reverse my thinking and attitude of getting frustrated so easily to prevent me from verbally lashing out and being sarcastic.

Through prayer, I came up with three key concepts to help me regroup: renewing, reflecting, and reminding myself.

I first started by renewing my mind. One of my favorite scriptures is Romans 12:2 (KJV): "And be not conformed to this world: but be ye transformed by the renewing of your mind, that ye may prove what is that good, and acceptable, and perfect, will of God."

To change my mindset, I had to regroup first by changing my prayers. In doing so, I added more quiet time with God. My routine also changed. I added additional fellowship, in which I attended more Bible studies. I joined a Biblical book-reading women's group. I did all of this because I wanted a different perspective on how God sees me.

In addition, I wanted and needed to continue to build my relationship with my heavenly Father by continuing to grow. I no longer wanted the routine and religion. I wanted a deeper relationship than I previously had before my trauma.

I had to learn differently. After I got angry with someone, I had to question myself and tell myself that I was better than my behavior and that I was created to do great work. My behavior needed to reflect Ephesians 2:10 (NKJV): "For we are His workmanship, created in Christ Jesus for good works, which God prepared beforehand that we should walk in them."

No matter what the textbooks say, behavior and attitude problems are part of a brain injury. Dr. Glen Johnson, a clinical neuropsychologist, in his traumatic brain injury survival guide, says people will accept that head injury can change your thoughts and memories, but have difficulty understanding that it also changes your emotions. Your emotions don't exist in some cloud that follows behind your head. They're in your head just like everything else.

Two of the more common changes in emotion are anger and depression. Someone may have been a "hothead" or angry before their accident. Since the head injury, this person's anger is multiplied two or three times.

Anger after a head injury is quite different from "normal" anger. Anger following a head injury tends to have a "quick on" and a "quick off." You can be in a good mood until something irritates you and you suddenly get angry. But this anger doesn't last; you're angry for a few minutes, someone changes the topic of conversation, and you quickly stop being angry. In another variation of anger problems, some little thing sets you off, and the whole day is ruined. In other words, you're not mad, you just seem in a bad mood.

I listen to what God has to say and be taught, corrected, and trained in righteousness when I read the Bible, which is the Word of God. Second Timothy 3:16-17 (NKJV) says, "All Scripture is given by inspiration of God, and is profitable for doctrine, for reproof, for correction, for instruction in righteousness, that the man of God may be complete, thoroughly equipped for every good work."

Day by day, God's word was planted deeper into my heart and his love started to grow and flourish inside me. I started having peace that felt so good inside.

Now, on many occasions, I will sit and listen to the birds outside singing and I will ask myself, 'I wonder what they are singing about?' God says to me, "They are singing to you about how much I love you."

After listening to the birds, I'm reminded of Mathew 10:29-31: "Aren't two sparrows sold for a copper coin? And not one of them falls to the ground apart from your Father's will. But the very hairs of your head are all numbered. Do not fear therefore; you are of more value than many sparrows."

Each day I am reminded how much my heavenly Father loves me as his daughter and that I am precious to Him. My walk and attitude have changed. I am now singing a new song.

WORKSHEET

Take action and journal about how you can celebrate your successes.

CHAPTER 21

Overcomer

"I'm a fighter, I will not give up, I will stumble and I will fall, but I will stand back up. It might take longer at times but I WILL stand back up and keep fighting." - Author Unknown

When trauma occurs, sometimes you might stumble and get knocked down. But getting knocked down doesn't mean defeat. Sometimes you have to rearrange your current situation and seek the guidance of our heavenly Father to help you keep fighting. My severe trauma required me to FIGHT (Faith, Inspiration, Greatness, Hope, and Triumph).

Regrouping after any type of severe trauma, faith is a major part of the recovery process. Faith allows you to keep fighting even when you don't know how the fight will end. But with God on my side, I am always a winner.

Mark 10:27 says, "But Jesus looked at them and said, 'With men it is impossible, but not with God; for with God all things are possible.'"

My greatness comes from knowing that, with God, I can conquer any battle I have to fight. I depend on God for everything and not man. God has been with me from the beginning and He'll be with me till the end.

Another key component is inspiration. During the times when I kept being hit with different situations and I wanted to hang my head down, I found inspiration and gratitude in the simplest things.

I AM a fighter. During my tough times, sometimes I will stumble and I may fall, but I will stand back up. I will not give up, because my greatness comes from God. God gave me the courage to be strong. God's Word in Deuteronomy 31:6 (NKJV) says: "Be strong and of good courage, do not fear nor be afraid of them; for the Lord your God, He is the One who goes with you. He will not leave you nor forsake you."

Bible gateway NKJV 2 Corinthians 5:7, which says, "For we walk by faith, not by sight"

> *Bible gateway NKJV Romans 15:13 says: "Now may the God of hope fill you with all joy and peace in believing, that you may abound in hope by the power of the Holy Spirit.*

Courage is a powerful weapon that kept me strong during many fights. On several occasions, I had to move to a different facility and wasn't aware of, or familiar with, the new environment. God was always with me. I don't get down for long. I WILL stand back up and keep fighting to keep the faith. Since I lost the vision in my right eye, I focused on 2 Corinthians 5:7, which says, "For we walk by faith, not by sight."

When darkness tried to keep me down and I felt defeated, I came back stronger, because I always had hope. Just like Romans 15:13 says: "Now may the God of hope fill you with all joy and peace in believing, that you may abound in hope by the power of the Holy Spirit."

My severe trauma was a hard and long fight but, because God is on my side, I have triumphed. My inspiration came from the Word of God. God gave me the greatness that's inside of me so I had nothing to fear. When life tried to knock me down, I never stayed down for long. I made sure I kept fighting and, because God was on my side, I had the victory. If and when trauma happens, keep the faith and find inspiration because greatness is inside of you. Always have hope so you can be victorious. Even though you may have to regroup and adjust to your circumstances, God is always with you to wipe away the tears and help you bounce back to make a greater comeback. You may hold your head down, which I did on many occasions, but I always felt the hand of God lifting my chin to remind me to FIGHT (Faith, Inspiration, Greatness, Hope, and Triumph) and never give up because you ARE a winner!

www.ingramcontent.com/pod-product-compliance
Lightning Source LLC
Chambersburg PA
CBHW042335150426
43194CB00005B/166